The Impossibility of Art Education

edited by Geoff Cox Howard Hollands & Victoria de Rijke

in the National Curriculum

The Impossibility of Art Education
edited by Geoff Cox, Howard Hollands & Victoria de Rijke

A **Camera*words*** publication
Volume 3

First published in 1999 by
Camerawork
121 Roman Road
London E2 0QN

Printed in UK by Spider Web

ISBN 1 871103 13 4

THE IMPOSSIBILITY OF ART EDUCATION

contents: p.

ACKNOWLEDGEMENTS:

Thanks to the Art staff and students at St. Paul's Way Community School; to Camerawork and Middlesex University's Centre for Research in Education, Arts, Language & Learning, for jointly funding the publication; and to all the contributors. Thanks also to Hatice Abdullah, Fabienne Cotte, Pam Meecham, Janice McLaren, Virginia Nimarkoh, Jane Sillis, Rebecca Sinker, Ken Taylor, Sophie Weeks, 1998 PGCE Art & Design students, Middlesex University.

Some of the ideas contained in this publication are recycled; they are based on previous working practices (such as *This is Not the National Curriculum for Art*,[1] Middlesex University 1994, and the aptly named *Recycling the National Curriculum*,[2] Camerawork 1996), and a draft education policy for Camerawork Gallery, London (unpublished and unfinished). The additional detail that Camerawork has since had their revenue grant from the London Arts Board cut by 100% (its state subsidy all but erased) presents the glorious irony of presenting an apparent 'failed' model of 'good' practice as the object of inquiry. In this sense, these projects and the publication are at odds with the present climate of the 'exemplification of standards'. Recognising that compromise and contradiction are the very stuff of art education, the key words in the title of the book: 'impossibility' and 'art/education', are to be taken as contingent terms.

Recent changes in cultural and education policy might be seen as a further backdrop to some of the ideas in this volume that attempt to simultaneously work with and against the predominant practices and orthodoxies of arts education. There is undoubtedly a currency for popularising approaches to Art with populist notions of increased access reflected in schemes such as *New Audiences* and the National Lottery's condescendingly titled *Arts4Everyone*, administered by the Arts Council of England. In the summer of 1997, the current Government's interest in the 'Creative industries' became apparent.

1.  2.

Tony Blair was quoted in *The Guardian* newspaper as saying: "I believe we are now in the middle of a second revolution, defined in part by new information technology, but also by creativity"[3]. The creative industries are estimated to be worth £50 billion to the economy. The Design Council, in a report for the Prime Minister, said: "the sector is growing at more than twice the underlying rate of the economy and is creating jobs faster"[4]. This vested interest is further reflected in the establishment of the Government's 'Creative Industries Task Force' followed by the 'National Advisory Committee on Cultural and Creative Education'[5].

There are a range of art/education constituencies currently involved in the debates about what Arthur Hughes calls a "re-conceptualising of the art curriculum"[6]. Although these discussions have been hastened by the proposed revisions to the National Curriculum, the real momentum has been the gradual realisation that the current art curriculum has little meaning for teacher or learner. Despite this, it is unlikely that the revisions to the National Curriculum will properly face this question and little will change.

Critical initiatives are coming from a number of directions such as the 'National Society for Education in Art and Design', the Arts Council/NSEAD focus groups, and the Arts Council of England Education and Training Group who established the 'National Arts Curriculum Task Group' as an inter-arts working party. Similarly, a range of publications have belatedly attempted to apply 'critical postmodernism' in the questioning of art education orthodoxies: intending to: "attack wrong-headed ideas, criticise sterile orthodoxy, and suggest ideas or policies for change".[7] Clearly there is 're-conceptualising' to be done, but the worrying aspect of all these debates is the lack of involvement of teachers in schools and the extent to which theoretical questions are not able to draw upon

3. Tony Blair, *The Guardian* newspaper, 22nd July 1997.
4. Ibid.
5. NACCCE, chaired by Professor Ken Robinson from Warwick University.
6. Arthur Hughes, *Broadside 1*, University of Central England, 1998.
7. Ibid,, *Broadside 1*. The NSEAD has produced a *Manifesto for Art in Schools* which draws upon many of the current debates. Others include the forthcoming publication, *The Art Curriculum and the Postmodern World*; the earlier, "Post-it Culture: Post-modernism and Art and Design Education", Stuart MacDonald, *JADE*, 17 No3; the editors of this volume offered, "An Impossible Art Education Manifesto", drastically edited for, *Engage*, issue 4, Spring/Summer 1998.

school practice. This is where this publication aims to situate itself as working with and against even the mainstream '(post-) modernisers'. Undoubtedly, anything with the word 'education' in close proximity is a contested ideological conjunction; from Antonio Gramsci's theory of 'hegemony' to Chief HMI (Her Majesty's Inspectorate) Chris Woodhead's latest DFEE (Department For Education & Employment) directives. What further compromises are in operation in these rapidly changing times of literacy drives and the increasingly peripheral role ascribed to the arts in formal education?[8] In arts organisations, there is still the complacent tendency to place education in a subsidiary role to gallery work and/or as cynical, upwardly-mobile, 'audience-development' activity and/or as an extension of commodity-culture. Conversely, it is argued that good educational practice in art should be supported by galleries with state and/or corporate arts funding, providing access through its education departments to those who would not otherwise appreciate the delights of contemporary art; who need exposure to diverse practices that supplement the inadequate canon of the National Curriculum. This is all very well, but it is as if there is something inherently and necessarily 'worth-while' about art in itself, failing to appreciate that culture is far more eclectic, inclusive and dynamic than mere art/education.

Nevertheless for this publication, which aims to focus on art/education, an attempt is made to undermine subdivisions that make education and art quite separate entities, claiming that art education is almost a contradiction in terms. There remain important questions to ask about the function of art as education as well as education as art.

The publication refers to a short arts education project with GCSE Art students from St. Paul's Way Community School, London E3.

8.

This project was perhaps unusual in not taking a thematic approach or using a child-centred method or drawing overtly on popular culture, as some of the more influential art education projects have in the past. Instead it attempted to use Modernist traditions (not Postmodernist!) and orthodoxies of 'formal' art teaching, to produce a critical practice; resisting the 'fashion' to use 'new media' in favour of the 'old media' of charcoal, paper and erasers. Working with this 'material reality' of the art classroom, these materials are clearly invested with technique, values, and skills that are highly institutionalised in the material apparatus of the school as a whole, and formal arts education. The intention here is to encourage reflexive practices in the school art syllabus as a means of integrating critical practice into practical project work, particularly through traditional formalist[9] exercises (through observational/ 'objective' drawing); to encourage a questioning of what form the art object might take in a material sense (from the found-object to the non-object).

What is proposed is a model not of 'good practice' but an argument for using art, any kind of art, as a means of exploring ideas and concepts of relevance to wider cultural experience. In this way, the intention is to question the 'hierarchies of knowledge' at work in the ways we see and understand art in 'message environments' such as galleries and art syllabi. Given that the majority of students studying art at GCSE level will not, could not, or would not even want to be artists, art presents the opportunity of learning critical skills in a way that might be more easily transferable to other cultural contexts. In other words, critical studies in art might usefully enable an understanding of other 'textual' systems and situations.

The publication asks: what useful connections might be drawn between/across these fields of art/education? Tim Brennan's *Material Histories* and Victoria de Rijke's *Titlepiece* refer to the performative aspect of pedagogy. For example, Tim delivered the material histories standing on a chair in what he calls the 'Sergeant Major' or what Victoria's definition of education calls the 'android' voice of the archetypal teacher. Appreciating the irony of this works

---

9. By 'formalist', we are drawing attention to the over-emphasis of the formal qualities of an artwork. This approach is problematic in that it suggests that meaning is simply encoded and that decoding reveals a pre-existing content. We would emphasise that form/content co-exist.

subliminally, counter to the explicit didacticism of a deliverable curriculum that results in testable evidence, or 'learning outcomes'. This is the impossibility that Howard Hollands describes in *It's Impossible*, where art education practice must affirm the canon of the National Curriculum, and the canon (through its Ofsted policing) that in itself determines good practice. As David Davies points out, in *Still, you don't have to be bright to do art. It's talent that counts*, 'radical' projects don't necessarily translate well in the classroom, either in terms of students' previous experience, or in an inner-city multicultural context. Nicholas Addison, in *Rub Out? Appropriation and Pastiche in the Art & Design National Curriculum* goes further in his recommendation for caution, given the risk of cultural erasure or threat to the students' 'construction of self' he sees as crucial to art education practice. Geoff Cox's *Be Realistic: Demand the Impossible* emphasises that present trends are not irreversible, and that central to these issues of domination are the interlocking apparatuses of culture and education. The extract from Alan Sekula's *School Is a Factory*, originally written in 1980, still serves to underline "what most everyone gave up on long ago, or more likely never even considered: namely to construct concrete instances of the possibility of cultural production within a renewed definition of the politics of the public sphere."[10] The claim of *The Impossibility of Art Education* is that making an artwork in reverse *can* reveal some of the political contradictions inherent in the institutions of art education.

DESCRIPTION OF DRAWING/ERASING EXERCISE

A group of sixteen year 11 GCSE students[11] from St. Paul's Way Community School were asked to select an area to draw in the artroom.[12] Although there was a formal 'still life' arrangement in the

10. Benjamin H.D. Buchloh, *Artforum*, January 1997, although this refers to Allan Sekula's practice.
11.The students were Rukshana Begum, Sultana Begum, Jolil Uddin, Qoyes Ahmed, Rajia Begum, Brian Stewart, Hasna Begum, Shubead Miah, Minara Begum, Abdul Hussain, Saleha Akthar, Sydul Islam, Hira Miah, Honufa Bibi, Poly Begum, and worked in School with Tim Brennan and Geoff Cox from Camerawork, October - November 1997.
12. The teacher began the term with observational drawing exercises using black and white materials investigating positive and negative space. This would usually lead to collage work and eventually to relief sculpture during the course of the term.

centre of the room, the students were allowed to choose anything but this usual focus of attention. They selected a range of objects and spaces: from paint pots to drawers for paper to the doors of the room itself. Students then used masking tape to the same scale as the paper to identify the exact area of choice. They were then asked to make a heavily detailed 'observational' drawing of this using charcoal. Students photographed stages of the production of the drawing at regular intervals. When these drawings were sufficiently detailed, the students were asked to rub them out. Again they were asked to record this process with photographs. They were encouraged to trace the charcoal marks as if running a video in reverse mode. In parallel to this, the students were given a short 'material history' of charcoal, paper and erasers. After they had completed the exercise,[13] Rauschenberg's *Erased de Kooning drawing*, of 1953, was cited as a precedent for their activity and to substantiate the activity itself as 'art-work'.

13. For the purposes of this publication, the aim is to focus on the simple exercise of making and erasing the drawings, although the students spent a day at Camerawork gallery engaged in a range of activities: reflecting on their work, mounting an exhibition as a way of marking the 'work' involved in gallery practices, writing commentaries directly on the walls (see note 30, p.36), and tracing their figures onto the walls (see note 23, p.61). The gallery was empty when they arrived. It should be noted that no one in the group had ever visited an art gallery before. The workshops were taken by Tim Brennan, Victoria de Rijke, Howard Hollands, and Virginia Nimarkoh, Camerawork, December 1997.

**Robert Rauschenberg,
Erased de Kooning Drawing, 1953**

drawing: traces of ink and crayon, on paper, in gold-leaf frame
19 x 14.5 inches (sheet size)

TITLEPIECE:
THE[1] IMPOSSIBILITY[2] OF[3] ART[4] EDUCATION[5]
Victoria de Rijke

1. **The** definite article is the only one in English, originating from Late Old English forms like 'thiu' or 'thou'. English is unique in having one form for singular, plural and all genders; suggesting perhaps a neutral, objective, non-judgmental, non-heirarchical culture? It can be stressed suggesting a superlative form: 'THE impossibility', meaning the worst, the best, the only impossibility. One of the impossibilities of Georges Perec's novel *La Disparition (A Void,* 1969*)* which has no 'e's in it, is that in French it can only have feminine articles and in English no definite article at all.

2. **Impossibility**; the 'im' a negative auxiliary, a prefix denoting 'not', the 'possibility' an Old French word which stems - if I may use that metaphor - from potency. It may be used as an abstract noun and the subject of a verb, though there is no verb in this title; the 'doing' is for you, the reader, the practitioner.

Jacqueline Rose's use of the word in her book *The Case of Peter Pan or The Impossibility of Children's Fiction* of 1984, is as a challenge to the mythical construct of literature that is written by adults ostensibly about and often for children, whilst all the time concealing itself as a desperately nostalgic myth to sustain adults. Rose's argument is that children's literature simply cannot exist in real terms, given children have almost no hand in it, and adults have so much at stake in it. Can children's art really exist for the same reason, or is that too an impossibility?

John Berger's use of the word in his 1969 essay "Magritte and the Impossible" (in *About Looking,* 1980), is to explore the artist's vision of his work as the material signs of the freedom of thought. As Magritte put it: "Life, the Universe, the Void, have no value for thought when it is truly free. The only thing that has value for it is Meaning, that is the moral concept of the Impossible". Berger goes on to admit that "to conceive of the impossible is difficult", and cites Marcuse defining art as 'the great refusal' of the world as part of the struggle to find a language to express what cannot be articulated. Describing a Magritte of a landscape seen out of a window and painted on a canvas in front of the window, he asks: "Is it possible/impossible that when the canvas moves, we shall see that behind where it originally was there is no landscape at all: nothing, a free blank?"

Whenever we have a symbolic structure - such as art or education or art education - it is structured around a certain blank, or void; it implies the foreclosure of a certain key signifier (like what 'art' is) we may know what it is not; it's not a pile of bricks, it's not a scribble, and so on. Although the school pupils who worked on this project were at a school that later received 'Visual Arts Specialist' status, they had not been to an art gallery before, though galleries were within walking distance. Why not?

Given everything we experience leaves a trace like the erased drawing, or the exhibition that went before, like a memory, (and crossing something out often draws more attention to it, by not being there), education is arguably there even more, when only a trace is left. When Freud's father died he realised the importance of memories and dreams, saying "I felt unable to obliterate traces of the experience" (letters to Fleiss, Nov. 1896). Death cannot be represented in Freud's unconscious but only imprinted, by "spacings, blanks, discontinuities..." and yet it is what we most desire to articulate, to fill the void. Freud saw the unconscious as an extra-ordinarily complicated mess, and yet as the essential component for humans coming to terms with the terrible mess of life. Psychotherapy was not seen as a cure from insanity to normality by Freud, only a means of moving from neurotic suffering to everyday unhappiness.

Writing, according to Derrida, after Freud, is communication with the absent, the reverse of speech, which is rooted in presence. Some writers have played on this - in Nikolai Gogol's short story of 1836 *The Nose*, the hero, a smug, ambitious Major, looks at himself in the mirror one morning and discovers he has lost his nose, and there's just a blank space left where it used to be. He searches the streets for it and finally discovers it - in the form of a whole object - a civil servant, in fact.

Is this nose a metaphor? If metaphor is where something stands for something else what does this nose represent? What might we imagine in place of the blank where the nose used to be? Is it a sexual symbol? Set free in the streets, what might a Major's nose do? Is it Gogol's castration complex? Much has been written about this nose, as you might imagine, not least because the story was censored in Gogol's time by the State, on the grounds that the nose visited a Cathedral. (Gogol had to make the nose visit a shopping arcade instead.) What if the nose visited an artclass in school? What if the nose became an art teacher, an education minister?

Nikolai Gogol was a sickly, ugly child, laughed at for his clumsiness at school, and nicknamed "the mysterious dwarf". He was particularly unpopular with his teachers, who constantly recorded his lazy, stubborn and disruptive behaviour. Gogol soon began to retaliate against his tormenters by spiteful and deadly convincing mimicry. Beware of the blanks in the system in which you are complicit, all of you who consider yourselves educators. Bear in mind that in Philip K. Dick's Sci-Fi novel *Do Androids Dream Of Electric Sheep?* (or to those of you who view rather than read, in Ridley Scott's film *Bladerunner*), the super policeman hired to terminate androids masquerading as real human beings, nearly mistakes a teacher for one. A teacher taking a group around an art gallery, in fact.

"Many people had turned out for the exhibit, including a grammar school class; the shrill voice of the teacher penetrated all the rooms comprising the exhibit, and Rick thought 'That's what you'd expect an android to sound -and look- like'."

Nicholas Paley's recent book on experiments in contemporary education and culture, *Finding Arts Place*, 1995, bemoans the erosion of the personal in these days of increasing bureaucratic hoop-jumping. What is a teacher but another mixed-up individual, after all? How could a common national curriculum possibly be delivered, unless educationalists were androids?

3. The Old English preposition '**of**' denotes the relationship to the noun possessor, generally used with certain adjectives and participles, such as 'terrified of'. 'The Impossibility of' is something of an artificial conjunction, but no more so than representing art and education together as if a single compound noun.

4. **Art** in its oldest French meaning has little to do with what's in the National Gallery: it means 'put together', 'join', or 'fit'. Hence the use of the word as a prefix such as 'artless' meaning natural, without guile, unskilled, devoid of skill, and 'artful' meaning artificial, cunning, crafty.

There was originally no visual education as part of the seven arts, until the C16th. When Hamlet gets frustrated with talking rather than doing he snaps "more matter with less art". Any reading we make of it is only ever art in part.

Raymond Williams (in *Keywords*, 1983) thinks our contemporary use of 'Art' began with Wordsworth's letter to a painter in 1815 where he wrote in a strange blend of missionary zeal and snobbery: "High is our Calling, friend, Creative Art". Art, 'calling' and matter came together in the C19th with works of art as prized commodities, and critics like Ruskin proclaiming that "industry without art is brutality". No wonder the worst slush of our times was produced in that era. Given the enormous influence of the notion of the over-priced genius upon us, could we ever re-make a shared ideal of the 'cultural worker'; educator and artist as one?

And what of the art of transgression? Is the artist in education a true subversive, or just someone who makes even less money than a teacher? Is the mark of a successful (rich) artist someone who holds education and teaching in contempt?

5. **Education** from the Old French and Latin word 'Educe' meaning to lead or draw forth, bring out what is latent, develop, has an essentially humanist goal: to facilitate growth that is physical, mental, social and emotional. It has been said that 'education is experience made significant', and one of our most significant experiences is learning that schooling has very little to do with education. In his 'deschooling' notion of education, Ivan Illich (*Deschooling Society*, 1971) might equally be defining art education's manifesto: "... to begin always anew, to make, to reconstruct, ... to refuse to bureaucratise the mind, to understand and to live life as a process - live to become...", or what bell hooks calls "education as the practice of freedom" (*Teaching to Transgress*, 1994).

Taking all of my etymological interpretations, the title "The Impossibility of Art Education" might easily be reworked into the words: "Thou Impotency Joins what is Latent" which sounds more like an accusation of sexual failure. Has state education failed to connect what is latently creative libido in its pupils? Given the strictures of disciplined citizenship, national curricula, testing, tables, funding, must it not it deliberately fail to offer the freedom Magritte saw as so vital? If the pupils win, the school will lose, and Chris Woodhead is the figurehead of zero tolerance. Thus bureaucratic impotency represses what might be seen as latent creativity or resistance.

Surely, the only kind of art education that is viable is political, personal, collective, and critical? - though, as Howard Hollands says "the possible takes a long time, the impossible even longer" - If Art Education is Impossible, then as Bismark remarked; "Die Politik is die Lehre vom Möglichen" (politics is the art/education of the possible).

19

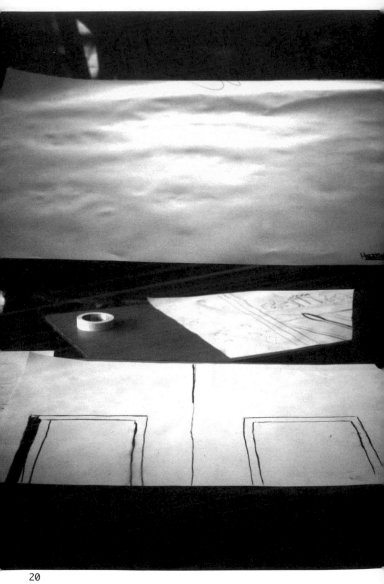

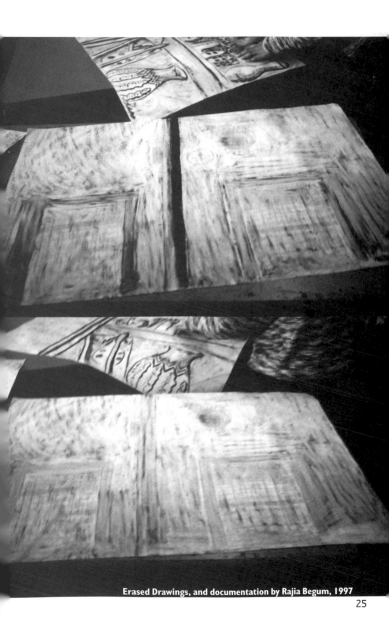

Erased Drawings, and documentation by Rajia Begum, 1997

BE REALISTIC, DEMAND THE IMPOSSIBLE [1]
Geoff Cox

The 'impossibility' inherent in all art education is that the value of the information supplied as well as the artistic competence it encourages is always discredited in advance. It might be simply reiterated that art education only serves to underwrite established values and expertise and that the art produced within educational situations is always discredited as necessarily amateur practice. For access to art through art education is always subject to the relations of production of art that thrives on strict categories of appreciation, leaving art education in the service of, and affirming art's exclusivity. The function of art education is generally untenable as it generally fails to acknowledge its own function in hierarchies of knowledge, taste and 'distinction'. And yet, how is value ascribed in these contexts and what useful connections might be drawn across these fields of art and education?

Both art and education express wider social relations within competitive systems with specific logics or rules. Bourdieu, in *Distinction*[2] acknowledges this uneasy link between art and education as fields of 'meaningful action', where symbolic (economic and cultural) capital is accumulated, in turn accounting for distinctions of value and taste. In this symbolic system, people perform their work and play activities according to organised principles of action; by for instance, either frequenting galleries and museums or not, as the case may be. These processes are largely hidden and reproduce established class structures in what Bourdieu calls 'pedagogic action' (in the art class-room, for instance). This model serves to stress that it is the interactions of artists, cultural producers, teachers, students, audiences and institutions in highly mediated situations (of production and reception) that contribute to these dubious pedagogic actions.

---

1. Surrealist slogan.
2. Pierre Bourdieu, *Distinction: a Social Critique of the Judgment of Taste*, (197
Routledge & Kegan Paul, 1984.

The overriding educational experience, and experience of a work of art tends to be one of deference to a single voice of authority. This 'listening' may not be passive necessarily (as clearly the hearing, reading and viewing subject has her/his own interpretative agenda too) but still might give the general appearance of passivity all the same, like a 'still life'. The overall structure and organisation of space is one that is designed to authenticate the single god-like speaker at the front of the teaching room, standing whilst everyone else remains seated, or the elevated 'still life' in the centre of the artroom around which everyone focuses their attention and reproduces as faithfully as they can. The intention is to legitimate the speaker's or artwork's authenticity and accept their authority by means of a particular set of learnt arrangements.

However, these relations, of the teacher/taught and student/learner, artist/subject and audience/object, are not fixed and need not reflect authoritarian politics (this relationship between authenticity and authority is a central concern of Walter Benjamin's artwork essay, where he argues that technical reproduction throws such orthodoxies into question and that new technologies might be used in a politically progressive manner). Changes in technology have the potential to be more democratic, but importantly this exists as potential and is why the reverse is often the case under advanced capitalism.[3] As an aside, an uncritical enthusiasm for 'new media' (such as the current 'National Grid for Learning') forgets that *all* media 'mediate', and that 'old media' such as charcoal, erasers and paper also operate within particular cultural and technological conditions. For instance in the international arena, Olu Oguibe is keen to point to material realities and contradictions of the 'virtual' classroom by describing problems of access in post-civil war Liberia: "There were no computers in schools. There were no schools at all".[4] How does this compare to the availability of adequate drawing materials? In the case of the technologies of mark-making, the example emphasises the symbolic meaning-making of the paper, charcoal, eraser, artroom, school, syllabus, the

---

3. This is argued by Walter Benjamin, in, "The Work of Art in the Age of Mechanical Reproduction", in, *Illuminations*, Fontana 1992, written in German in 1935/36. [also http://www.obsolete.com/artwork]
4. Olu Oguibe, "Forsaken Geographies: Cyberspace and the New World 'Other'", in, *Annotations 3: Frequencies, investigations into Culture, History and Technology*, inIVA 1998, p.24.

teachers, the artists, and of course the artist-students themselves. All these are issues of emptying and filling objects, spaces and events, and of course minds.

MAKING AN ARTWORK IN REVERSE

In *Erased de Kooning Drawing* of 1953, Robert Rauschenberg literally erased a drawing by the celebrated Abstract Expressionist Willem de Kooning, thereby removing its aesthetic content. Rather than use one of his own drawings, in which case "the work would return to nothing",[5] it was important that the drawing already had a commodity value. It needed to be physically difficult to rub out in such a way that the act of erasing it would be laborious and be a symbolic rejection of 'formalist commodity-making'. Rauschenberg's own description was "to purge myself of my teaching and at the same time exercise the possibilities".[6] Significant to its translation to an art classroom context is the spatial mapping of the activity itself adapting "the angle of imaginative confrontation; tilting de Kooning's evocation of a worldspace into a thing produced by pressing down on a desk".[7] According to this source, the flatness of the desk opens up possibilities like a workbench "referring back to the horizontals on which we walk and sit, work and sleep"[8] making the artwork part of everyday activity perhaps, or at least the standard practices of the art classroom that are often poorly adapted formal teaching rooms.

Such a blatant example of reversing the production procedures of an artwork is rooted in contemporaneous 'zero-action' events and 'auto-destructive' art. Relevant too is its inverse mode, the 'auto-generative' art object as the object that makes itself automatically. The Surrealist interest in automatism aimed to stimulate spontaneous creative activity, and to diminish the significance of the artist, making 'found-objects' like the Dadaist 'ready-made'. Duchamp famously explained that everyday objects, 'readymades' became works of art as soon as he said they were,[9] since nothing is

---

5. Robert Rauschenberg, Smithsonian Institute catalogue, 1976.
6. Ibid., p.75.
7. Leo Steinberg, "Other Criteria: The Flatbed Picture Plane", in, Harrison & Wood, *Art in Theory: 1900-1990*, p.951.
8. Ibid., p.951.
9. Marcel Duchamp, "The Richard Mutt Case", in, Ibid., p.248.

owned or original; if tubes of paint are manufactured, even paintings are readymades according to this logic and would prove difficult to attribute and value. This is confirmed in that "Dada means nothing" and that "there is a great destructive, negative work to be done".[10] The many manifestos of both Dada and Surrealism prove useful models of good practice in the art classroom in preference to the official (National Curriculum) Manifesto for Art, in their desire to change social conditions and transform everyday reality; to turn the impossible into the possible perhaps.

The most notorious example of zero-action is perhaps the no-sound or silence of John Cage's *4'33* (composed 1952). The performer, who simply sits quietly in front of the piano for four minutes and thirty-three seconds, merely opens and closes the piano lid to indicate the piece's three 'movements'. This emphasises that either nothing is an echo of something, or as Cage put it: "Every something is an echo of Nothing".[11] Arguably following the principle of the readymade, Cage, in fact writing on Rauschenberg, transposes his belief that any noise exists as potential music: "and everything, a pair of socks, is appropriate, appropriate to poetry, a poetry of infinite possibilities".[12]

The zero-action attempts to remove representation and signifying practices but is knowingly (or is it annoyingly?) aware of its necessary failure. The active audience is encouraged to reflect upon the 'mediating' devices of the work of art and consider the distinction between presentation and representation; it has to be remembered that even the representation (the sound, the word, the image) is not the thing itself. Yet, despite the apparent engagement with a politics of representation, it is ironic to note that Cage was a 'quietist', in that he did not demand political change only a critique of established value judgment. If part of the concern of the dematerialised art object was to emphasise representational process and performative elements (we might think of drawing performances, endurance drawings, etc), it is as if the process itself

10. Tristan Tzara, *Dada Manifesto* 1918, in, Harrison and Wood, op cit., p.249.
11. From, John Cage, "Silence", from *Lecture on Something*, p.131, quoted in Frances Dyson, "The Ear That Would Hear Sounds In Themselves", in, Kahn & Whitehead, *Wireless Imagination*, MIT Press 1992, p.383.
12. John Cage, "On Rauschenberg, Artist, and his Work", in, Harrison & Wood, op cit., p.719.

has become the material that is the centre of attention. It follows that the dematerialised artwork is a way of shifting attention to other representational processes like talking, writing, and actions which result in the making of meaning. What matters is how they are organised and regulated within particular institutional arrangements.

THE MAKING EVENT

Applying this formulation, there is no impossibility as such, only context and the medium employed as the message or the art object/event. Furthermore, as an object/event, its meaning is activated by the presence of a viewer through a 'making-event'.[13] The viewer is encouraged to make meaning or expressed differently to become the artist to fill the void of meaning. The viewer makes the work through granting it meaning reinscribing it with detail as if drawing it on a blank sheet of paper.

Undoubtedly, the structures of any environment convey controlling messages to those who work or participate in it. In drawing attention to the ways in which the structure or process of the (medium) environment manipulate the (message) perceptions, senses and attitudes (into McLuhan's soundbite "The Medium is the Message"), the question might become: how are these spaces (the classroom, gallery, this book) organised and to what effect? For instance, in terms of lesson plans and structures, the activity of the teaching room is conventionally broken down into content and method. It is often imagined that content is disseminated through the lesson itself and that the method carries no content; why else separate them in such a way? This is a particularly subtle and effective form of control. As the contents of lessons are rarely remembered, what is being learnt but the structure of the learning? This is the overall message as outlined by Postman and Weingartner in *Teaching as a Subversive Activity*.[14]

There might be a number of motivating factors for exposing the mediating apparatus in the art classroom, not least to retain the

13. John Latham's phrase, from, *Dialogues with the Machine*, ICA conference, June 1998 - although he, in fact, distinguishes between a 'making-event' and 'viewing-event' - something I would not wish to do.
14. Neil Postman & Charles Weingartner, *Teaching as a Subversive Activity*, (1969), Penguin, 1975.

possibility of changing it. After all, what is really going on in any classroom but an over-determined state conspiracy! This is the 'functionalist' model of the school/gallery as a factory engaged in the production of repressive values, dominant ideology, social divisions of labour, and so on. Allan Sekula employs this analogy productively when he claims: "If school is a factory, art departments are industrial parks in which the creative spirit, like cosmetic shrubbery or Muzak 'lives'."[15] This pedagogic factory is heavily stratified to reproduce a workforce who are highly unlikely to become artists or even consumers of art for that matter. Recent and plentiful state intervention seems to confirm this functionalist view that schools are factories concealing their ideological workings. In this way, a photograph of a factory or school[16] tells us next to nothing about the institution or of the relations of production therein.[17]

This bleak scenario stands in stark dialectical contrast to the emancipatory educational practices of, for example, Freire's *Pedagogy of the Oppressed*,[18] who called for students to act rather than be acted upon. The suggestion to 'throw a spanner in the works' so-to-speak, suggests there is some possibility for change in the system. For example, the artist John Latham's proposal for

15. Allan Sekula, "School Is a Factory", in, *Photography Against the Grain: Essays and Photoworks 1973-1983*, Halifax: Press of the Nova Scotia College of Art & Design, 1984, p. 228. See p.81, this volume.

16.

17. Here I am paraphrasing Brecht: "the situation is complicated by the fact that less than ever does the mere reflection of reality reveal anything about reality", quoted by Walter Benjamin, "A Short History of Photography", in, *One Way Street and other writings*, Verso 1985, p.255.

18. Paolo Freire, *Pedagogy of the Oppressed*, Penguin 1980, inspiring many others in its wake; ideals more recently reiterated in, Phil Cohen, "Negative Capabilities: On Pedagogy and Post-Modernity", in, *Rethinking the Youth Question: Education, Labour & Cultural Studies*, MacMillan 1997, p.386.

British Leyland (as part of the Artist Placement Group's work in/with industry) was to get each worker on the production line to make one mistake as a (auto-motive) creative act.[19] Here and elsewhere, the (Fordist) production process is crucial in that people make meaning within meaning-factories even if they are alienated from their labour. Similarly, if the learning environment is used to make people the objects of its system rather than encourage social action, then there is critical content to be discovered in the analysis of method and process. It follows that the unhelpful distinction between form and content evident in formalist drawing exercises should be erased.

MAKING REFERENCE IN REVERSE

If, as has been argued elsewhere, contemporary art practice in schools could be periodised as around 1956,[20] all is not lost. For one thing, this offers an appropriate critical strategy to work within the established parameters of practice rather than impose a 'preferred', better, more contemporary one as this would seem counter-productive. It might easily be argued that there is no better place for critical studies than with reference to the established art canon that many teachers already work with (including formalist drawing exercises, for instance). However progressive the alternatives may seem, their effectiveness is what counts.[21]

Modernism's most useful elements are often discarded in the name of a critique of its conception of progress as if progress itself is 'bad' practice like the parallel rejection of 'progressive education'. It is often forgotten how a history of modernism is also a history of modernism's internal critique of the institution of art. There are many examples of artists who have mounted critiques of the nature of exhibitions by, for example, including the work of amateurs and children, mocking the establishment through what appears to be on one level a replication of day-to-day activity in the art classroom. In a period when education is subject to heavy state intervention,

---

19. Referenced by, Barbara Staveni, *Dialogues with the Machine*, ICA conference, June 1998.
20. Pam Meecham, *The Impossibility of Art Education* research seminar, Middlesex University, July 1998.
21. This is what David Davies challenges in his essay, "Still, you don't have to be bright to do art. It's talent that counts", this volume, p.71.

contemporary art in schools might do well to heed some modernist practices in this regard as a critique of art's own institutionalisation (and this is certainly not to say that those naughty boy-artists Jake and Dinos Chapman exhibition of school examination artwork is a case in point).

Evidently culture does not advance in a straight linear fashion, but as Hal Foster puts it, moves in 'screw-turns' or 'spiral-like' patterns.[22] By rejecting a vertical or horizontal axis, he says it is possible to reject an 'avant-gardist'[23] break with the past for the maintenance of historical and social axes. This kind of approach is easily overlooked and allows for a return to the past where appropriate to open up present, even future contingencies and possibilities. This question of historical returns is a well-worn tactic and runs the risk of mere stylistic mannerism of postmodernist pastiche. Like Marx's generalisation that 'history repeats itself, first as tragedy then as farce', the fear is that perhaps this project (along with the farce of much of contemporary art) is a mere pastiche of the erased drawing. There is a confusion over parody and pastiche as both involve imitation and mimicry. Parody mimics style which mocks or ridicules the original, though sometimes affectionately. Pastiche likewise imitates a particular style but does so without an ulterior motive. Fredric Jameson says "Pastiche is blank parody, parody that has lost its sense of humour... blank irony"[24] as pastiche begins where parody is no longer possible, impossible even.

Responding to the ways in which radical forms are incorporated/co-opted into the system, or the ways in which those in power construct its oppositional practices, Foster some time later than *Postmodern Culture* (1985, in "Whatever Happened to Postmodernism?" 1996) borrows the idea of 'deferred action' (from Freud) to point to the "relation between turns in critical models and returns of historical practices".[25] In this way and in turn borrowing

22. Hal Foster, *The Return of the Real*, MIT Press 1996. This is similar to Bruner's spiral theory of learning.
23. Note: the 'avant-garde' is loosely defined as those artists and writers whose techniques and ideas that are experimental and radical, in advance of those generally accepted.
24. Fredric Jameson, "Postmodernism and Consumer Society", in, Hal Foster, *Postmodern Culture*, Pluto Press 1985 , p.114.
25. Hal Foster, "Whatever Happened to Postmodernism?", in, *The Return of the Real*, op cit., p.207.

from Benjamin ("Each epoch dreams the next... but in so doing it revises the one before"), he rejects the notion that Postmodernism is a distinct break or departure from Modernism as some commentators would have it (so if parody is possible it would make an erased drawing not 'blank irony' after all). This is a departure of sorts from Foster's earlier work that argued for Postmodernism as a critical practice resisting dominant narratives and the canon. His aptly titled *The Return of the Real* contributes to the argument that it has become uncritically commonplace to privilege the 'politics of the sign' over the 'sign of politics'. Under the force of 'progressive' capitalism, it appears that dissent too has become commodified. One answer is to frame the questions differently rather than fall into mere opposition that is easily deferred as 'other', or that crudely reproduces dominant forms of address.

MEANINGFUL ACTION

In "The Author as Producer", Benjamin argued that social relations are determined by the relations of production and therefore artists should try to transform those relations.[26] To merely make political artwork is not enough in itself, artists should attempt to change the(ir) means of production and supply a progressive model of arts practice. He claimed that "an author who has carefully thought about the conditions of production today... will never be concerned with the products alone, but always, at the same time, with the means of production. In other words, his [sic] products must possess an organising function besides and before their character as finished works".[27] To merely work as an "ideological patron" on behalf of the oppressed without due attention to the production process, he says, is "an impossible place" to be.[28]

Such lack of attention to 'meaningful action' is reflected in the under recognition of pedagogic work in arts practice, or at the very least, the lack of awareness of the pedagogic implications of artwork. When either the artist or the artwork claims to be political in content, this further serves to echo Benjamin's point of a lack of progressive form. Reflecting their own narrow education, artists are

---

26. Walter Benjamin, "The Author as Producer", (1934), in, *Understanding Brecht*, Verso 1992.
27. Ibid., p.98.
28. Ibid., p.93.

notoriously easy to deflect from their function as teachers. For instance, the conflicts associated with artists' residencies in schools often reflect these competing creative and disciplinary tensions: of reactionary artists who think they should not be teachers working alongside teachers who are often artists too. Clearly part of the difficulty here are the archaic and conservative approaches to arts production, and teaching for that matter, as individualised practice. It would seem that both fields should embrace more participatory and collaborative work with people and machines.

It was Lautréamont who claimed: "Poetry must be made by all; not by one" proposing collaborative experimentation in creativity and automatism. There are numerous precedents here within a history of conceptual art practices that place emphasis on the 'work' of art as opposed to the 'object' of art, placing emphasis on the making activity as opposed to the singularity of the commodity itself. These conceptions might serve to firmly undermine the unhelpful clear distinction between artist and teacher and those liberal institutions that perpetuate its cozy departmentalisation (schools, gallery education departments, funding bodies and the like). For instance, following the idea that any object in a gallery might function as an artwork, what if any activity could be taken as artwork too? The students from St. Paul's Way Community School simply wrote comments on the white walls of Camerawork gallery (December 1997).[30] There are precedents here, like artist Guilio Paolini, in, *At Last Alone* (1980), who 'performed' a work of art quite literally, drawing on the walls of the gallery. Similarly, students of Nova Scotia College of Art & Design working from John Baldessari's initial instructions, covered the walls in a repeats of the statement *I will not make any more boring art* (1971), as a parody of school punishment and the traditional copying of their art 'masters'.[31]

30.

31. According to Tony Godfrey, in, *Conceptual Art*, Phaidon, 1998, p.196.

If gallery education were to take place in an empty gallery would the activity of art education itself be seen as the artwork? Would it gain more cultural value? The work of Tim Rollins and K.O.S. is a striking example here of collaborative education practice that has been co-opted/bought into by the commercial art market. Moreover, despite any worrying contradictions inherent in their selling (out), the artist's claim is important in seeing the medium, not as painting or collage, but as *teaching*.[32] Perhaps the most obvious allusion here is to the artist Joseph Beuys who claimed, "to be a teacher is my greatest work of art".[33] In his projects like *The Free University*, education was taken to be 'social sculpture', the arrangement of argument and discussion to mobilise latent creativity.

Yet perhaps these examples privilege the 'progressive' artist when clearly culture is not handed down but made by people everywhere. This is what Paul Willis refers to as "grounded aesthetics". If, as Willis describes it: "The institutions and practices, genres and terms of high art are currently categories of exclusion more than of inclusion",[34] then learning should be centred on the school students' frame of reference. For all its weaknesses art education in school can be a key area which provides an opportunity for those students who, in a culture of social exclusion (the league table culture) find some value in making activities.

There is no directive as such in this essay, just the suggestion that it simply might be useful to explore some of the common-sense ways of appreciating art in order to investigate the process of making a 'work' of art within the school students' frame of reference: in their terms, it appears that the value of an artwork is inscribed through work/labour, is associated with things that look most 'real' and that clearly demonstrate skills. At first viewing, this seems consistent with an inclusive definition of cultural production that includes art, that sees art as a part of a broader category of culture and communication, and that recognises that art and education are commodities, have materiality, production processes, economies, markets, and so on. If the traditional curriculum validates formalist

32. Tim Rollins, *Imagined Communities*, conference, John Hansard Gallery & inIVA, May 1996.
33. Tony Godfrey, op cit., p.195.
34. Paul Willis, *Common Culture: Symbolic work at play in the everyday cultures of the young*, Open University 1990, quoted on rear cover.

'commodity-making', then critical concern should be in the conditions of its institutional formation. The link to process, although a common strategy in art teaching, might simply seek to emphasise that people operate within these systems of meaning-making and this might be recorded, described and reflected upon as an integrated critical practice. This is an invitation to question the institutional and discursive structures at work in art education; to encourage practitioners "to be 'troublemakers' in challenging the circumstances in which they work, exhibit, or teach".[35] There are objects produced, meanings produced, social relations and politics, within these systems of art and education that can be marked, rubbed out and redrawn if the appropriate critical skills are demonstrated.[36]

Art and/or Education are social practices that generate possibilities of revealing political contradictions inherent in the hierarchical structures of power and knowledge in the gallery/artroom. The point is to uncover how these representations (images, talk, texts, actions which results in the production of meaning) are organised and regulated within particular institutional arrangements. Is it possible to have a responsibility towards the use of materials and towards society in such a scenario? The drawing/erasing exercise was an *ironic* effort to reintroduce other possibilities, such as contingency and contradiction to the material apparatus of the school and formalist/functionary arts education. In returning to the slogan at the beginning of this essay, it seems all the more desirable to demand the impossible.

35. David Trend, "Culture and Pedagogy: Theories of Oppositional Practice", in, *Cultural Pedagogy: Art/Education/Politics*, Bergin & Garvey, 1992, p.12.

36 .

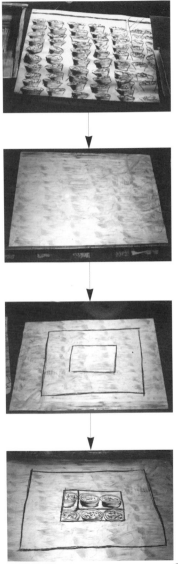

Erased Drawings, and documentation by Sydul Islam, 1997.

39

MATERIAL HISTORIES
Tim Brennan

PAPER [1]

"Paper was invented, before the Christian era, in China, a country where learning and the written word were valued highly. About 2,000 years ago a need developed there for a new writing material to replace the sticks of wood and bamboo employed previously. With the widespread introduction of a new writing implement, the brush, people began to write on silk. Compared with wood and bamboo, silk had the advantage of being light and pliable and an admirable vehicle for calligraphic script. But it had one disadvantage: it was costly.

... Tradition has it that the noble art of making paper was invented by a Chinese eunuch by the name of Tsai Lun. For he is the first paper-maker to be mentioned in Chinese history books. In 105 A.D. he reported to the Emperor Ho-ti that he had successfully produced a writing material from hemp, bast, discarded fishing nets and cloth. The Emperor greatly appreciated this ingenuity, and the new material was duly adopted. All we know concerning Tsai Lun's subsequent career is that he became embroiled in a court intrigue and, to avoid being put on trial, went home, took a bath, combed his hair and drank poison.

As regards the method of producing the pulp, we know that the raw material was beaten in stone mortars together with water. Mortars of this kind are mentioned in the story of Tsai Lun and the American paper expert Dard Hunter found similar mortars on his travels in China about 50 years ago. The same Dard Hunter is also convinced that the earliest sheets of paper were made by diluting the pulp with water until one obtained a fibrous slurry, which was then poured over a screen set up in a frame. The Chinese were expert felt-makers, a craft which may have enhanced their understanding of the

---

1. A continual process, an unbroken line of production that begins with the tree and ends with the cut sheet.

melting of fibres. Paper was used above all for the propagation of ideas." [2]

CHARCOAL [3]

"There is made of char-coal usually three sorts, viz: one for the Iron-works, a second for Gunpowder, and a third for London and the Court, besides Small-coals of which we shall also speak in its due place. We will begin with that sort which is usd for the Ironworks, because the rest are made much after the same manner, and with very little difference.

The best Wood for this is good oak, cut, and set in stacks ready for the Coaling, chuse out some level place in the Coppice, the most free from stubbs, etc. to make Hearth on: in the midst of this area drive down a stake for your Centre, and with a pole, having a ring fastened to one of the extreams (or else with a Cord put over the Centre) describe a circumference from twenty or more feet semi-diameter, according to the quantity of your Wood designed for coaling, which being near may conveniently be Chared on that Hearth; and which at one time may be 12, 16, 20, 24, even to 30 stack: If 12 therefore be the quantity you will Coal, a circle whose diameter is 24 foot will surffice for the Hearth; if 20 Stack, a diameter of 32 foot; if 30, 40 foot, and so proportionably.

Having thus marked out the ground, with Mattocks, Haws, and fit instruments, bare it of Turf, and of all other combustible stuff whatsoever, which you are to rake up towards the Peripherie, or out-side of the circumference, for an use to be afterwards made of it; planning and levelling the ground with the Circle: This done the wood is to be brought from the nearest part where it is stacked in wheel-barrows: and first the smallest of it placd at the utmost limit, or very margin of the Hearth, where it is to be placed longways as it lay in the stack; the biggest of the Wood pitch, or set up on end round about against the small-wood, and all this within the Circle, till you come within five or six foot of the Centre: at which distance you shall begin to set the Wood in a Triangular form till it come to

---

2. Bo Rudin, *Making Paper: a look into the history of an Ancient Craft*, Rudins, 1990, pp.15-16.

3. Family history tells me that my name, 'Brennan' is a corruption of the Old Norse or Icelandic, 'Brannan' for Charcoal Burner.

be three foot high. Against this again, place your greater small-wood, and all this within the Circle, till you come within five or six foot of the Centre: at which distance you shall begin to set the Wood in a Triangular form till it come to be three foot high. Against this again, place your greater Wood almost perpendicular, reducing it from the triangular to a Circular form, till having gained a yard or more you may pile the wood longways as it lay in the Stack, being careful that the ends of the Wood do not touch the Pole which must now be erected in the centre, nine foot in height, that so there may remain a round hole, which is to be formed in working up the Stackwood, for a Tunnel, and the more commodious firing of the pit, as they call it, tho not very properly. This provided for, go on to Pile, and set your Wood upright to the other as before; till having gained a yard or more you lay it long-ways again, as was shewd; And thus continue the work, still enterchanging the position of the Wood, till the whole Area of the Hearth and Circle be filled and piled up at least eight foot high, and so drawn in degrees in Piling, that it resemble the form of a copped brown Household-loaf, filling all inequalities with the smaller Truncheons, till it lie very close, and be perfectly and evenly shaped. This done, take straw, haume, or fern, and lay it on the outside of the bottom of the heap, or wood, to keep the next cover from falling amongst the sticks; upon this put on the Turf, and cast on the dust and Rubbish which was grubbed and raked up at the making of the Hearth, and reserved near the circle of it; and with this cover the whole heap of Wood to the very top of the Pit or Tunnel, to a reasonable and competant thickness, beaten close and even, that so the fire may not vent but in places where you intend it; and if in preparing the Hearth, at first, there did not rise sufficient Turf and Rubbish for this Work, supply it from some convenient place nearto your heap: There be who cover this again with a sandy, or finer mould, which if it close well, need not be above an inch or two thick: This done, provide a Screene; by making light hurdles with slot rods, and straw of a competent thickness, to keep off the Wind, and broad, and high enough to defend an opposite side to the very top of your Pit, being eight or nine foot; and so as to be easily removed, as need shall requiring, for the luing of your pit.

When now all is in this posture, and the wood well rangd, and closd, as has been directed, set fire to your heap; But first you must provide you with a Ladder to ascend the top of your Pit: This they usually make of a curved Tiller fit to apply to the convex shape of the Heap, and cut it full of notches for the more commodious setting of the colliers' feet, whiles they govern the Fire above; when now they pull up and take away the Stake, which was erected at the Centre, to guide the building of the Pile and cavity of the Tunnel. This done, put in a quantity of Char-coals (about a peck) and let them fall to the bottom of the Hearth; upon them cast in Coals that are fully kindled; and when those that were first put in are beginning to sink, throw in more fuel, and so from time to time, till the Coals have universally taken fire up to the top: Then cut an ample and reasonably thick Turf, and clap it over the hole, or mouth of the Tunnel, stopping it as close as may be with some of the former dust and rubbish: Lastly, with the handles of your Rakers, or the like, you must make Vent-holes, or Registers (as our Chymists would name them) through the stuff which covers your Heap to the very Wood, those in Rangers of two or three foot distance, quite round within a foot (or thereabout) of the top, tho some begin them at the bottom: A day after begin another row of holes a foot and a half beneath the former, and so more, till they arrive to the ground, as occasion requires. Note that as the Pit does coal and sink towards the centre, it is continually to be fed with short and fitting Wood, that no part remain unfired; and if it chars faster at one part than at another, there close up the vent-holes, and open them where need is: A Pit will in this manner be burning off and charing, five or six days, and as it coals, the smoke from thick and gross clouds, will grow more blue and livid, and the whole mass sink accordingly; so as by these indications you may the better know how to stop and govern your spiracles. Two or three days it will only require for cooling, which (the vents being stopped), they assist by taking now off the outward covering with a Rabil or Rubler; but this, not for the above space of one yard breadth at a time; and first remove the courest and grossest of it, throwing the finer over the heap again, that so it may neither cool too hastily, nor endanger the burning by reducing all to Ashes, should the whole Pit be uncovered and exposd to the Air at once; therefore they open it thus round by degrees.

When now by all the former Symptoms you judge it fully chared, you may begin to draw; that is, to take out the Coals, first round the bottom, by which means the Coals, Rubbish and Dust sinking and falling in together, may choke and extinguish the fire.

Your Coals sufficiently cool'd, with a very long-tooth'd Rake, and a Vann, you may lead them into Coal Wains, which are made close with boards, purposely to carry them to Market." [4]

RUBBER [5]

"[He] introduced me to Mr. E.E. Green, F.E.S., the government entomologist, and then led me to some of the fifteen-year-old Para trees, which we tapped. It was really too near the middle of the day for the latex to do more than ooze out very slowly. The tool used is well known. It only needed a very few cuts with it, however, to convince me of its usefulness; indeed, for the Hevea it is far superior to any form of machete that I have seen. The incision is really a drawing cut that takes out a strip of bark, laying the cambium bare. The cut is clean, small and may be made by the most unskilled coolie with but little chance of injuring the tree. I had with me a small two-bladed tapping axe, invented by a friend in the United States, which I had brought along to test. We all tried it, but the simple little tool far outdistanced it. Leaving the collecting and straining of the latex to the coolies, Mr. Carruthers took me to his bungalow for breakfast, which meal occurs at noon, and there we discussed various phases of rubber planting." [6]

4. John Evelyn Sylva, or a *Discourse of Forest-trees, and the Propagation of Timber in His Majesties Dominions* (as it was deliverd in the Royal Society the XVth of October, MDCLXII) Jo. Martyn & Ja. Allestry, 1664, pp.100-102.

5. The British scientist Joseph Priestly, observing its ability to rub out pencil marks, gave rubber its English name. Its name in French, 'caoutchouc' is from the Indian-American 'cachchu', 'the wood that weeps'.

6. Henry C. Pearson, "What I Saw in the Tropics", *A Record of Visits to Ceylon, The Federated Malay States, Mexico, Nicaragua, Costa Rica, Republic of Panama, Colombia, Jamaica, Hawaii, India*, Rubber Publishing Company, 1906, p.39.

It's Impossible

It's impossible to tell the sun to leave the sky,
It's just impossible
It's impossible to ask a baby not to cry,
It's just impossible.
Can I hold you closer to me
And not feel you going through me,
But the second that I never think of you?
Oh, how impossible

Can the ocean keep from rushing to the shore?
It's just impossible.
If I had you could I ever ask for more?
It's just impossible.
And tomorrow, should you ask me for the world
Somehow I'd get it, I would sell my very soul
And not regret it for to live without your love
Is just impossible
Oh impossible,
Impossible,
Impossible
Impossible [1]

THE ERASURE OF POTENTIAL

"Knowledge is predicated on the necessity of its erasure."[2]

Secondary teacher of art:
"Now, I want you to forget everything you have done in primary school."

---

1. Elvis Presley, "It's Impossible", on the album *Fool*, words and music by Wayne - Manzanero.
2. Sawad Brooks, "Digital Erasure", (1998), http://www.thing.net/~sawad

Art foundation course lecturer:
"Now, I want you to forget everything you have done at secondary school."

Higher education professor of art history:
"We are always suspicious of degree applicants who have studied Art History 'A' Level at school. We prefer those without that kind of knowledge."

One of the few benefits of the National Curriculum has been an attempt to strengthen progression between phases of education, to try and make sense of these gaps, to move away from the denial of all that has gone before, to reflect and build upon each phase. It is easier to blame what has gone before, than what is not going on at present. It is the culture and competitive climate of the marketplace that undermines these transitional relationships. Blame-and-shame defines the space between the rungs on the educational ladder. The trauma and negativity which characterises each space implicates everyone in the process; the pupil, the teacher, and the parent/carer.

Access, no access. Entry, no entry. Winners, losers. Success, failure. The emphasis is on the gate, doorway or hurdle, not the path between. Product, not process. Negotiating the space of the door-frame is the test to determine access from one place to the next. It can mean the erasure of potential, equality and opportunity.

THE ERASURE OF CREDIBILITY

The question frequently put to secondary art teachers: "Do you still find time to do your own work?" underlines a perceived opposition or contradiction between art and art education. Bernard Shaw reinforced this credibility gap with a phrase which time has yet to erase:
"Those who can, do, (produce art), those who cannot, teach (art)." (My parentheses). Teaching as *not* doing according to Shaw.

The gap between contemporary art and school art is underlined when the art graduate starts an Art & Design teacher training course,[3] and has to change role from being artist to teacher of art.

---

3. interested appplicants please phone 0181 362 5000
or email admissions@mdx.ac.uk

Just what is this difference? How can the art/design/craft experience form the basis of their teaching when 'school art' has remained essentially the same for the last fifty years?[4] The enforcement and reinforcement by the National Curriculum is demoralising. The shock and disappointment for the artist/student is less to do with the quality of work in school than the nature of the work, and the low expectation. "We would like you to do colour wheels with them", is one phrase heard recently. What are colour wheels for these days? They are mostly a form of torture, to which the poor pupil is strapped until they can render something akin to the primary secondary colours with twenty-year old powder paint. This is not only an erasure of previous experience but of contemporary culture too. We can see how the process becomes self-fulfilling in terms of the negative attitude of higher towards secondary education. The role of the foundation year at art school is to liberate the student from the perceived stranglehold of school art.

GOOD PRACTICE, THE CANON, THE SYNOD AND THE POLICE

It is when we hear the term 'good practice' in relation to art in the primary and secondary phases that we shudder. We do not hear much about 'good practice' in the art schools. This is the language of quality control.[5] What constitutes 'good practice'?

Good practice is what fulfils the canon of the National Curriculum now in the hands of QCA (Qualifications and Curriculum Authority); the Synod. Good practice in the form of the canon is enforced through inspection by OFSTED (Office for Standards in Education); the police.

Bad practice is a form of transgression (i.e play, forbidden by OFSTED). Good practice affirms the Canon, which in turn determines itself as good practice.

Perfect symmetry? Art and education are not always symmetrical.

If the term *art* ceased to be used, was itself erased, then this problem might also be erased along with many of the activities

---

4. Arthur Efland, "The School Art Style: A Functional Analysis", *Art Education*, National Art Education Association, 1976.
5. The author worked in 'Quality Control' for *Birds Eye* frozen peas one summer and was aware of the precedent being set. The peas which did not pass through the holes of maximum/minimum dimensions or were declared too dense (sic) were rejected as falling short of the required standard.

currently justified in the name of *art*. We are sliding towards this kind of reform. The canon in art meets the canon in education, with the potential for a new meaning given to critical studies. One way forward might be to critically examine the nature of the art education framework in school and the gaps or relationships between this and the wider world of visual culture. The national discussions now underway are the ones that teachers were not permitted to have prior to or during the development of the National Curriculum.[6] This discussion is still largely dominated by higher education and subject advisors. Where are the teachers in this process?

THE ASSESSMENT GAP

GCSE and 'A' Level Art assessment criteria have recently been revised in an attempt to encourage and accommodate the unsafe, the risky, the unorthodox. One way put forward by the London GCSE Examinations board has been to expand the range of so-called basic elements in art and design to include, alongside the traditional "line, tone, colour, texture, form", etc., new 'elements' such as "comparing, criticism, describing, expressing ideas, justifying preferences, talking, writing". We might well ask how or why these can be considered 'basic elements' of art; why indeed we still use this term, given there is no explanation in any syllabus. Perhaps these questions will hasten the day when the 'basic elements' in art are made redundant, as they suggest a misconception of a common language of art. Contradictory definitions of the so-called elements are to be found in numerous art education publications, which absurdity is compounded by the fact that this new broader definition above does not exist at Key Stage 1, 2 or 3 or indeed at 'A' level. The difference now is that the assessment emphasis in art has to shift from outmoded notions of skill solely tied to these basic elements. There is a need for a recognition that the intention of the learner is reflected in the way the work is 'read' or assessed, to shift from product to process. This development was in fact well underway in some schools, prior to the imposition of the National Curriculum and its accompanying grip of assessment.

---

6. These discussions have been taking place in a vairiety of contexts; NSEAD (National Society for Education in Art & Design), The Arts Council of England, QCA(Qualifications & Curriculum Authority).

Art has been required to fit the assessment model, not the other way around. As a recent "Thought for the Day" on *Radio 4* suggested, it is the measurable which becomes important, rather than seeing how the important can be measured. The drive for measurement, comparability, accountability and cost effectiveness (i.e. league tables), has increased standardisation and pressure for the amalgamation of examination boards. Ironically, in this consumer-led climate, choice is not an option when it comes to the curriculum, except in the private sector! It is evident that many schools with successful results at GCSE and 'A' Level have found a formula for success (for success results, read league tables) and teach to the test. The lack of any framework for curriculum innovation, such as used to exist through the Schools Council means that research and development is almost non-existent. The canon cannot cope with innovation.

THE NECESSITY OF ERASURE: HOW TO ASSESS THE RUBBED OUT DRAWING?

Erased drawings 1997 by the GCSE group from St Paul's Way School.
Erased de Kooning drawing 1953 by Robert Rauschenberg.

Rauschenberg requested that de Kooning give him one of his drawings in order that he could erase it and thus claim it is as his own. It took Rauschenberg one month and forty erasers to rub out the thick crayon, grease pencil, ink and pencil markings. Is the effort involved here important in order for Rauschenberg to author it? Duchamp would simply have claimed the de Kooning as his own without the gesture of struggle. Rauschenberg's act draws attention to process as a creative act and the role of the individual in this process. This is also an issue for GCSE and assessment.

The St Paul's Way children erased their own drawings under instruction from teachers. In this latter sense the project is no different from any other didactic drawing exercise. Where does the intention come from? Is it re-running the traditional model to critique itself at the instigation of the teacher, rather than the child? Given the philosophy of the London GCSE as outlined in the following statements from the *1998 Training Pack for Moderators*:

"Studying Art is Art in Education... Making Art is Art... Any attempt to write Art specific criteria will result in dictating content. The examination depends upon three interactive concepts:
• Process: the method by which something is done
• Progression: forward movement within an activity
• Development: growth sideways and in depth within an activity
It is a mistake to think this means a particular way of working, a formula. "[7]

Yet the exam boards still retain the framework to assess GCSE and 'A' Level art under the headings of discrete practices such as textiles, graphic design, three-dimensional design and so forth, despite the fact that the assessment criteria are common to all practices. Why? There is plenty of anecdotal evidence from external moderators to indicate that schools developing a successful formula in terms of examination grades will be under pressure not take risks, particularly when entry to further or higher education may be at stake.

The GCSE moderator arriving at St Paul's Way School Art Department this summer will be confronted by a number of erased drawings as part of the complete submission by each student. The moderator will be expected to look for evidence of self-directed learning and the intentions of the candidate, and be expected to apply the definition of process in the *GCSE Art Syllabus*, "the method by which something is done". There is clearly a critical/ conceptual dimension being addressed through the skills/basic elements aspect. This is one model of critical-making. What factors are involved for the assessor and moderator in the case of St. Paul's Way? The role of the moderator for GCSE is to confirm that the assessment has been carried out in accordance with the assessment criteria and not to mark the work. The moderator will be guided by the Head of Art.

• why were the drawings/erasures done in the first place: for fun, to develop skill, to draw attention to process, to set up expectations, to undermine, to challenge?
• is the drawing/erasure the independent work of the student?
• how is the skill in the drawing/erasure to be measured?

7. *GCSE Moderator Training Pack*, London: Edexcel, 1988.

• how successfully has the student achieved their intention?
Whose intention?
• how does intention change/become modified in the process?
• how has the art department assessed the erased drawing in their internal assessment, have they brought something of their own to the process?
• what is the nature of the evidence in relation to intention? The exam board encourages teachers/moderators to search the sketch-book/critical study for evidence if it is not explicit in the work. Dialogue is vital.

How might a contemporary artist such as Sawad Brooks who has produced some digital work about erasure, reflect on the process?

"We 'draw' on the screen by drawing the mouse over the table top. Traditionally, we would draw a stick or soft material to leave an incision or deposit on a surface. This was direct - or so it appears today. The concept of directness continues to be important in how we design interfaces. Directness connotes proximity: The shortest distance between two points is a straight line. Technologies are often understood as mediating our experiences of the world. Radio, television, cinema, photographs. Such technologies are also very often understood as substitutes for our natural form of communication: speech. In being substitutes, it is said that they distance us from nature. Sticks and pencils are rarely considered to be technological, at least not high-tech. But pencils (and other pigmentation tools) mark the technological basis of drawing: the deposit (left as the drawn mark) is a visible substitute when touch alone will not leave a significant mark.

Digital media is permeated with the language of erasure, and yet, the meaning of erasure of digital records differs from the meanings erasure holds in relation to analog media. In analog media, when something is erased, it is often possible to sense the mark left by erasure. Thus Rauschenberg was able to present his *Erased de Kooning* drawing as his own (ironically). Erasure leaves its own traces, it is writing or drawing. It is a wiping clean which puts forth an order with the possibility of decipherment. How do we decipher the static of digital erasure?

I make drawing interfaces to draw upon the erasure of erasure in the realm of the digital. Is there a digital realm? Would not its limits as realm condition its identity? Can drawing an object over a surface remain significant as an act of depositing, of leaving, of loss and gain? Or will it become another gesture significant of something entirely other?"[8]

In exactly the same way as the moderator viewing the GCSE work in the school, the viewer of *Erased de Kooning drawing* needs to be aware of the context for the activity. In which case does this become part of the work? We only know it to be an erased de Kooning drawing because we are told so. We only know it to be art because we are told so, but surely this applies to all art. Rubbing out a Leonardo would be a very different kind of erasure in the same way that Duchamp putting a moustache and beard on Leonardo's *Madonna of the Rocks* would raise very different questions to the amended *Mona Lisa*. Man Ray's suggestion to use a Rembrandt as an ironing board, another form of erasure, would not have the same resonance if it were a Van Gogh. Some of Van Gogh's paintings were in reality used as floor boards, unaware of their impending status or value as art! There is a suggestion by Philip Fisher that Rauschenberg was parodying the act of *effacing* as a primary act of art making "... he does not go on to use the ground he has cleared and levelled. He rests his case in the negative position."[9]

The Rauschenberg is an act in response to the de Kooning, in the context of the abstract expressionist gesture. Is the fact that the response overlays or removes the de Kooning simply a particular outcome of this act or an extension of the de Kooning, or both? Does the work at St. Paul's Way extend this further? The process is the endless product.

"When he erased a de Kooning drawing, exhibiting it as *Drawing by Willem de Kooning erased by Robert Rauschenberg,* he was making more than a multifaceted psychological gesture; he was changing - for the viewer no less than for himself - the angle of imaginative confrontation; tilting de Kooning's evocation of a world space into a

8. Sawad Brooks, "Digital Erasure", (1998), http://www.thing.net/~sawad
9. Philip Fisher, *Making and Effacing Art*, Harvard, 1991, pp.98-99.
10. Leo Steinberg, from, "Other Criteria", (1972), in, Harrison & Wood, eds., *Art in Theory: 1900-1990*, Blackwell, 1992, p.951.

thing produced by pressing down on a desk."[10]

In *Art and Language Paints a Picture*:

"Direction: Starting from the top-left hand corner, (1) and (2) spread Nitromors, an ethylene-chloride based paint stripper, on the painting. They scrape it off, exposing bare canvas. An erased, incompetent Augustus John. Somehow it doesn't have the frisson of Erased de Kooning."[11]

If definitions in art education are really closures or containers, therein lies liberation. However, the greatest external container now is that of economic/ideological control of the curriculum. Art education is moving into uncharted waters, trawling for the critical tools to guide it to a mooring in the reconceptualised curriculum.

As a result of something so simple and so absurd as a school timetable (use a timetable as an ironing board) art in the primary school has been overwhelmed by the measurement of literacy and numeracy and in the secondary school it has to be accommodated within 50-minute segments between geography and PE. This is impossible, but one alternative scenario might be worse; art education may no longer take place in school. It could be rubbed out, erased altogether. If it were to be removed from the timetable, it might re-emerge positively through other fields of study. Other subjects, however, have their own problems. Art needs institutional frameworks as much as they need art, because art helps define these frameworks in terms which usually lie outside the parameters of that institution. This is the contradiction, an impossibility for art education.

MIND THIS GAP: THE ERASURE OF THE SPACES BETWEEN ART & EDUCATION, OR SQUATTING?

Rachel Whiteread might well have taken a school or gallery and turned these spaces inside out rather than *House*.[12] The significance would have been overwhelming. Make them go outside to play. Whose school or whose gallery would this then be? What fills these spaces, psychologically and physically?

---

11. Michael Baldwin, Mel Ramsden and Charles Harrison, *Art and Language Paints a Picture*, 1982, in, Ibid., p.1027.
12. Rachel Whiteread, *Untitled (House)*, 1993 - since destroyed.

What happens when we cross the threshold from street to gallery, from street to school? Possibly/impossibly, those who can, will explore the gap, that space between art and education. Spaces created by institutional frameworks. These spaces are sometimes occupied and defined by artists. This gap is reinforced by those who see art in education as something different to art elsewhere, perhaps of less value than, say, art in the wider community. The values differ. These values are reinforced through the assessment frameworks. Move beyond the school gates and the assessment regime no longer applies. Yet art moves in and out of school. Schools are not only security conscious as far as the physical well-being of children is concerned. Risk assessments are carried out under health and safety but also with the curriculum. Curricular security and safety is essential with OFSTED hanging around like the bully outside the school gates. On the other hand, there are many artists/students of art who despise pedagogy and the teaching profession because they believe it to be incapable of doing justice to the creative potential of individuals. These two entrenched positions refuse to talk and recognise what they have in common.

OPEN MINDS, OPEN DOORS

Open Minds, Open Doors; the slogan on Teacher Training Agency publicity, evokes John Berger's *Ways of Seeing* in that: "the relation between what we see and what we know is never settled... there is this always-present gap between words and seeing."[13]

Marcel Duchamp illustrates this problem well.

11 Rue Larey,[14] made in 1927, utilised one door hinged to two different frames opening on to two different spaces. When closed to one space it was open to another and vice versa. The door in a closed position was also in an open position. Impossible, or perhaps the door was simply not open as opposed to closed. When is a door not a door? When it's a-jar. Keeping your options open.

In 1961, a replica of Duchamp's door and frame was shown in a gallery and destroyed at the end of the show.

In a 1963 exhibition in Milan, a life-sized colour photograph taken of the original door still in its Paris location was shown. The original door was then moved to New York. The photograph was

13. John Berger, *Ways of Seeing*, Penguin/BBC, 1972, p.7.
14. Marcel Duchamp, *11 Rue Larey*, 1927.

mounted on a wooden board and signed and dated by Duchamp: "Marcel Duchamp, Milan, 1964".

In 1963 in Paris, another door replaced the original one bought by the New York Gallery.

In Duchamp's final work *Étant Donnés* of 1946-66[15] two peepholes are positioned in two old doors transported from France, in order to view the setting beyond one viewer at a time. The arrangement emphasises what cannot be seen. What lies outside or beyond? What is the nature of the gap between what we see and what we know? It is the same with art in the classroom? Whose space? Whose display? Should the art room be an art room or a room in which art is produced? Is it a gallery or a workshop, or both?

The St. Paul's Way pupils working in the 'empty' space of Camerawork Gallery, responding to the absence of work and in most cases to the absence of a notion of what a gallery is, began to define the space through a variety of activities. This included consideration of the door between street and gallery and what happens as they move from one kind of public space understandable in terms of shops, traffic and people involved in all sorts of activity, and the space inside the gallery to do with something called 'art'. The group created cut-out clones of themselves pointing out of the window at the street, or attached to the automatic sliding glass door. They depicted themselves defining this new space.[16] There are some who see the space of the art room in school as different, an oasis, a haven. What changes? Does art do this?

Why do we hear pupils say that the work produced for 'A' Level art is the art that they are required to do, and their other work is their own, is valued and has meaning for them? There is a change in conceptual space here, which has a resonance in the physical space of art room, gallery, and the worlds beyond.

Is this an impossibility? Isn't this the door we came in?

---

15. Marcel Duchamp, *Étant Donnés* (1946-66), one of his final works, produced in secret, now in the Philadelphia Museum of Art.
16. See images overleaf. For school artroom doors, see pp.20-25 .

Opposite page: a8e: drawing/erasing, Shubeaa Miah, 1997 '.

RUB OUT? APPROPRIATION AND PASTICHE IN THE ART & DESIGN CURRICULUM
Nicholas Addison

• an art teacher's 'good' advice in the form of an instruction:
Rubbers may only be used to render a form; no erasure.

• an art teacher's explanation of negation:
Rub it out only if you understand why you are doing so.
Rub it out for me.
Rub it out because I say so.

• an imaginary pupil's objection:
Strange, I've been rubbing out my work for years and the teacher usually gets cross with me.
She says, "Don't you value your work?"
I say, "NO".

• an imaginary student's objection:
You're asking me to rub it out!
I want to fill it in:
obliterate through accretion, decorate to extinction.
Decorate, decorate. Let me near a surface!

When, in 1953, Robert Rauschenberg requested a drawing from Willem de Kooning, a drawing he intended to 'reverse', he was paying homage to the artist who for a generation exemplified heroic aesthetic adventure. Harold Rosenberg, de Kooning's fervent champion, saw the new painting as the result of an "encounter", the canvas "as an arena in which to act":

"A painting that is an act is inseparable from the biography of the artist. The painting itself is a 'moment' in the adulterated mixture of his life - whether 'moment' means the actual minutes taken up in spotting the canvas or the entire duration of a lucid drama conducted in sign language. The act-painting is of the same metaphysical substance as the artist's existence. The new painting has broken down every distinction between art and life."[1]

His position assured, and acknowledging his cultural paternity, the older artist acquiesced: how could he otherwise? Rauschenberg's Oedipal compulsion demanded some form of resolution. The older man handed over a drawing. He handed over a 'good' one, so good it would test the younger artist's nerve. He handed over a dense one, as thick and knotty as the younger man's hunger.

It is supposed to have taken the young iconoclast six weeks, six weeks of painstaking, surgical erasure. Like some spectral doppelgänger caught in a glass he retraced the great man's every move; like a film played backwards he mirrored the veteran's actions in order to return. Was this painful for de Kooning, did he feel hurt? Anecdotal evidence would suggest he did. The young man's irony, his negative parody of art as action, his spiteful echo, hurt the older man to the very quick. If only the visual could be negated as easily as a proposition:

"Thus for every thought there is a contradictory thought: we acknowledge the falsity of a thought by admitting the truth of its contradictory. The sentence that expresses the contradictory thought is formed from the expression of the original thought by means of a negative word."[2]

Where is the visual equivalent of 'not'? So neat, so simple. She asserts, he disagrees. Symbolically, Rauschenberg's purge, the making of his 'tabula rasa', was the moment of de Kooning's death.

At a later moment an artist invites a group of young 'GCSE' Level art students to draw. They work variously, but with application. They produce large charcoal drawings, transforming the banalities of an empty room with their diligent looking and trust. Now they must rub them out, rub them out in homage to an old man. Back in 1953 his own rubbing out had signified a turning point:

1. Harold Rosenberg, "The American Action Painters" (1952), in, Charles Harrison and Paul Wood, eds., *Art in Theory: 1900-1900*, Blackwell 1992, p.582.
2. G. Frege, "Negation", in, P. T. Geach, ed. and trans. with Stoothof, *Logical Investigations*, Blackwell 1977, p.131.

"When in 1957 the critic Leo Steinberg telephoned Rauschenberg to discuss *Erased de Kooning Drawing*, of which he had heard rumours, he asked if he would appreciate it more if he actually saw it. Rauschenberg thought not. "'This was', Steinberg wrote, 'my first realisation that art could take on this new modality, spinning like a satellite through consciousness, rather than being physical fact.' Nevertheless, Rauschenberg thought enough of the drawing to put it in a gold frame."[3]

Forward to the empty room: what does the students' directed action signify? Must they in turn parody in homage to their guide's preferences? Must they live out his own deferred action, expunge the last vestiges of his projected expressivity, allow him vicariously to witness his own death? Pastiche is no longer reduced here to imitating the visually given of Modernism, "the power of the image to communicate itself merely as, colour, shape and texture",[4] but the imitation of process, the power of action to be revisited as ritual, in this instance a theatrical, dare one say spectacular, act of self-denial.

Foster makes much of 'deferred action' a process in which the current avant-garde critically revisit, deconstruct and reassess their predecessors:
"Taken together the notions of parallax and deferred action refashion the cliché not only of the neo-avant-garde as merely redundant of the historical avant-garde, but also of the postmodern as only belated in relation to the modern. In so doing I hope that they nuance our accounts of aesthetic shifts and historical breaks as well. Finally, if this model of *retroaction* can contribute any symbolic resistance to the work of *retroversion* so pervasive in culture and politics today - that is, the reactionary undoing of the progressive transformations of the century - so much the better."[5]

The 'impossible project' is, no doubt, one such attempt, an attempt to reinforce the counter-project by investing the art education of young people with a degree of critical self-consciousness, an attempt to force students to, "embrace problematic bodies of

3. Tony Godfrey, *Conceptual Art*, Phaidon, 1998, p.64.
4. Brandon Taylor, "Art History in the Classroom: a Plea for Caution", in, D. Thistlewood, ed., *Critical Studies in Art and Design Education*, Longman 1989, p.104.
5. Hal Foster, *The Return of the Real*, MIT Press 1996, p.xiii.

knowledge", confront and address "conflicting ideological values" and provide an opportunity to oppose "entrenched notions with some degree of revisionism"[6]. But the project to date comes perilously close to the millenarianism Foster warns against:

"But lest I render this second neo-avant-garde heroic, it is important to note that its critique can also be turned on it. If the historical and the first neo-avant-gardes often suffered from anarchistic tendencies, the second neo-avant-garde sometimes succumbs to apocalyptic impulses... As a result contemporary artists concerned to develop the institutional analysis of the second neo-avant-garde have moved away from grand *oppositions* to subtle *displacements*."[7]

Is rubbing out one such grand gesture? Rauschenberg's act, in its moment, was remarkably prescient, an emblematic action which ousted the old Europeans, exposed the rhetoric of male self-hood and creativity so beloved of the modernist project, and cancelled out the generational deference usually afforded the canon, however recently formed. But Rauschenberg didn't stop there. *Factum I* and *II* further parody this self-denial. The second, an 'exact' copy of the first, is a systematic imitation of his gestural catharsis and irreverently refutes Rosenberg's 'act-painting'. They are a deconstructive act, a binary opposition in which the original and the copy, the authentic and the fake, cancel each other out in mutual self-reference. In itself, the erased drawing had not been enough to convince Rauschenberg. Of what could this action convince the students? An action so intelligent, so sure in its historic specificity. It must surely mean something different when repeated, when revisited in this way?

The National Curriculum has validated, indeed valorised, the potential for mimicry in Art and Design in schools. If the intention has been to saturate the student in the early-modernist canon of popular art history, it is not the Impressionist critique of academic orthodoxy so much as the 'impressionist' virtuosity of postmodern parody that has been its guiding principle. Pupils and students learn to copy, transcribe, pastiche, parody, exemplary sources. Many are encouraged to adopt some technical or stylistic feature, for example,

6. M. Price, "Art History and Critical Studies in Schools: an Inclusive Approach", in, D. Thistlewood, op cit., p.114.
7. Hal Foster, op cit., p.25.

divisionist colour, Futurist fragmentation, and apply it to their own observations. I have stated elsewhere:

"With young children transcription is a revealing process because they select from the image to be 'copied' those things or features which hold most interest for them. At secondary level, with its analytical imperatives and tools, the process of transcription focuses on the more superficial task of the imitation of surface... Thus at GCSE, 'A' Level and GNVQ, the critical and contextual sketchbook is all too often a collection of transcriptions (some annotated), drawings and pamphlets from exhibitions, written personal responses to favoured images, extracts copied from art historical texts and serendipitous reproductions. It often possesses great energy and enthusiasm, seems to indicate visual investigation, but in truth has only its 'look': closer inspection reveals appropriation, imitation, material exploration and variation."[8]

In the advisory document *Exemplification of Standards*[9] SCAA reinforce this new orthodoxy suggesting that 'knowledge and understanding' can be achieved through the processes of analysis and quotation. From the evidence of the reproduced exemplars this would entail respectively, an imitation of formal elements and the ability to appropriate disparate features from a multicultural and multi-historical visual landscape. At least the impossible project asks students to adopt a conceptual and critical principle, that of negation, but it is applied technically through the mechanical process of erasure.

The evidence in schools is ubiquitous, the copy, the transcription, the pastiche, the parody, have become the legitimising signs for critical investigation from Key Stage 2 through to 'A' Level. No one wishes to belittle the educational role of these processes, but in a squeezed curriculum such activities should be subsidiary to the critical and contextual investigation that enables students to make sense of their own and other's production. Despite Thistlewood's heresies[10] and a developing literature, critical and contextual studies

8. Nicholas Addison, "Who's Afraid of Signs and Significations: Defending Semiotics in the Secondary Art and Design Curiculum", in, *The Postmodern Curriculum*, NSEAD 1999.
9. SCAA, *Consistency in Teacher Assessment: Exemplification of Standards, Art Key Stage 3*, SCAA 1996.

is at best a secondary observance servicing the primary concern of making. Hughes reiterates the increasingly urgent question:

"Why have we apparently excluded from the present the possibility of an art curriculum based upon the critical, contextual, historical, or cultural domains, and not predicated upon studio practice and the model of the artist?"[11]

Most teachers of Art and Design are reluctant to let go of this model. Their own education, most likely fine art based and steeped in the rhetoric of modernist autonomy and transcendentalism, may lead them to abjure the notion of the pastiche and the dependence on others that it presupposes, but educationalists, policy-making bodies, even examination boards, have been demanding a historical, critical and contextual dimension for years: teachers know they must pay obeisance to the law and the pastiche gets them by with the least possible effort. Once the pastiche project is over, pupils and students can return to their formalist exercises and orthodox representations. There are schools where a critical curriculum is encouraged, where the advocacy of a committed teacher persuades the external examiner that their students' work meets the examination criteria to the full; but these are few, and to change the culture of the art room requires extraordinary energy, dogged persistence and courts unpopularity if not mutiny.

The impossible project in many ways conforms to the studio model for it is an (art) ahistorical and thus decontextualised pastiche of a critical approach to production and its significance. It could be argued that the self-conscious appropriation of a process is a recontextualisation of historical practice; if so the significance of this particular exercise is the negation of the students' own production. How might a student from today's plural classroom receive this act of self-abnegation?

"One mark of oppression was that black folks were compelled to assume the mantel of invisibility, to erase all traces of their subjectivity during slavery and the long years of racial

10. D. Thistlewood, "Critical Development in Critical Studies" (1993), in, Dawtrey et al, eds., *Critical Studies & Modern Art*, Open University Press 1996.
11. Arthur Hughes, "Reconceptualising the Curiculum", in, *Journal of Art and Design Education*, vol. 17, no. 1, Blackwell 1998, p.48.

apartheid..."[12]

GCSE Level students follow courses which, in terms of their aims and objectives, invite them to develop skills which can lead to some degree of autonomy, a step on the way to self-actualisation, concepts steeped in the rhetoric of modernist utopianism. They are, however, expected to make this journey fully aware of the contexts, past and present, in which art has and is produced and received, including the multi and intercultural contexts of the UK's post-colonial existence. The celebratory multiculturalism of the 70s and 80s is slowly being superseded by anti-racist strategies that critically examine constructions of difference while acknowledging that essentialist tactics may be a necessary weapon of empowerment. Students construction of self, so carefully negotiated, that fragile balance between personal and social imperatives, might be threatened by the 'apocalyptic' gestures of others, not in knowing and understanding those gestures, but in imitating them to the point of self-denial, succumbing to the new coloniser's agenda of negation. Is this hysteria? The reformers are evidently well-intentioned. But has this directed act, this collective act of invisibility, traces of other less benevolent agendas?

Erasure is a dangerous critical tool. Caution is recommended.

---

12. bell hooks, "Representing Whiteness in the Black Imagination", in, L. Grossberg et al, eds., *Cultural Studies*, Routledge 1992, p.340.

STILL, YOU DON'T HAVE TO BE BRIGHT TO DO ART IT'S TALENT THAT COUNTS
David Davies

We who teach art are no strangers to requests for our services. Our antennae rapidly recognise the furtive sidling up of the head of drama needing a little favour to rescue the production values of the end of term performance. Don't we always find ourselves using the results of our art teaching to provide a decoration for parents evening or to prettify a dark corner of the school keeper's rest room or the temporary fence around the collapsed manhole in the scabby piece of ground called the outdoor recreation area? And for what reward? Maybe a couple of extra pots of powder paint and a promise to be allowed to complete the task undisturbed in our free periods with the help of a mutinous group of Year 11 pupils chucked out of everyone else's lesson as impossible to teach.

Still; everybody knows you don't have to be bright to do art. Its talent that counts. But does it?
So what exactly are we teaching in the time given over to art lessons? Is art at secondary school level something which is universally essential to the cognitive/aesthetic/social/political development of our students?
OR is it, like other curriculum areas, simply quantified through prescribed syllabuses and just another course to follow linked inextricably to the National Curriculum orders and exam boards syllabuses? Art as an esoteric/ aesthetic experience or GCSE, A level or GNVQ?

What then is art teaching about? What is this thing of value we give to our students: the vast majority of whom will cease their formal visual education at the end of Key Stage four? We are all aware that most students go on from secondary education into career routes other than art. So should we be more concerned with the development of skills which are vocational and transferable such as, the ability to learn independently, do research, solve problems or communicate effectively? Art can and does encourage the development of these skill areas and if taught effectively also provides an educational experience which challenges individuals to achieve highly through undertaking a personal exploration of the subject. I think successful art teaching values the aesthetic/ intellectual and the vocational equally whilst encouraging pupils to revel in the sheer pleasure to be gained from the practical making of art.

Hopefully my own art courses succeed through their content and structure to account for the various needs of my pupils. My aim is to encourage pupils in a pursuit of individual discovery, broadening their experience of the world through experiencing the process of art, reaching outcomes which are satisfying and which advance their understanding and knowledge of life. Pupils achieve highly if they have a clear understanding and real possession of their work and its methodologies, but more than this, they must also perceive the outcomes of their efforts to be of quality and therefore take on a personal value. Children first of all see the production of a satisfying product as prime objective of learning about how to do art. Bearing this in mind we must go further to engender an appetite in pupils which goes beyond making and engages a personal exploration of art and a questioning of why they are undertaking a particular course of study. The concepts, which underpin and enhance children's learning in art are then crucial to developing these higher levels of understanding what art is and why people do it.

Successful art teaching is a partnership between the practical and historical/critical. It must offer a teaching and learning strategy which challenges through the process of making, whilst encouraging positive questioning of concepts and ideas through research work, critical discussion and reflection. Thankfully most art departments have over the years applied some form of this strategy to their teaching. However to do this successfully, particularly the research based activities, often requires a level of resourcing which is currently denied many art departments. How many heads of art have adequate budgets for travel, ICT, reference books, CD-roms, artists in residence, etc? The point here is that to do art teaching successfully, money and support is as important as it is to any other subject. Many art teachers, whilst long becoming practised in arguing their yearly case with curriculum managers for the retention of existing levels of resourcing, seldom look wider than department capitation for their funding needs. So how has this come about and how can this situation be alleviated?

I think to some extent art teachers have undervalued their subject's contribution in education and have felt hesitant to go out and actively seek the resources their departments need. In this respect we should celebrate art's contribution to education as major. Let's recognise that art is one of the most successful subject areas in secondary schools. We should definitely not be hesitant to blow our own trumpet when looking for funding or support: there is money out there and organisations who really want to become involved with our success, we simply need clear strategies and the will to promote our work and basically go out and get it. In a way I suppose exam league tables have in some perverse way been a good thing for art departments in secondary schools in that they highlight the success achieved by pupils studying art. Across the country art consistently achieves a higher percentage A-C GCSE score than most other areas of the curriculum and many head teachers battling Ofsteds and DFEE 'naming and shaming' policies are now becoming much more aware of this. It would be interesting to ascertain how many schools in the country rely upon their art results to boost overall scores to acceptable levels. I would imagine there to be more than a few whose GCSE performance would be below the threshold for 'special measures' were it not for the efforts of their art departments in achieving high scores. Remember, the national average for C grade and higher in GCSE Art & Design is 62% where many departments achieve ten points or more above this level.

Equally perversely, at least up until David Blunkett's recent pronouncements on disapplication, the National Curriculum has also done its bit to focus management minds on curriculum provision for art. As a foundation subject we have been given parity with the likes of humanities, languages and PE. True: we then have to generate mountains of paper work to achieve real approval, but through this ordeal by paper we can sometimes begin to feel almost as grand as our more illustrious curriculum partners. We still have to fight the philistine element but that is increasingly becoming a thing of the past, (or is it?). The annual exhibition may be seen by all and admired by many, but unconvinced voices still murmur of a lack of intellectual or academic rigour in the subject. Our lack in promoting valid career pathways for pupils studying art also goes some way to reinforce this view. Its interesting to note that in London there are more jobs related to art & design than financial services. That fact answers the perennial question "Yes, but what job can you do with it?" Negativity about art as a valid subject is of course pervasive, (ask art teachers), and directly or indirectly can influence curriculum management decisions. It is therefore up to us as art teachers to take the initiative and encourage our line managers to value our subject and to even use art as a lead subject for the raising of achievement in other curriculum areas.

In my own school we have done just that. From my arrival as head of department in 1991 my colleagues and I have worked to raise achievement using a variety of strategies both inside and outside the classroom. Our methods have included developing 3D work, using artists in residence and promoting pupils work through exhibitions in school, galleries, business premises; indeed anywhere we are allowed to mount them. I firmly believe that these activities have enhanced the reputation of the department and have been major factors in taking our GCSE results from a low of 38% to the present 98% A-C with a fourfold increase in student numbers taking the exam.

Riding on the back of our success in 1997 we successfully applied to the DFEE for 'specialist school status' in visual arts. The attendant positive publicity and increased funding has enabled the school and the department to develop further and offer a wider range of courses to our students and returnee learners both during the school day and in the evenings and weekends. Other subject areas are now working with the department to develop cross-curricular projects and also submitting independent proposals which will allow them to access arts college resources, develop their own curriculum areas, whilst also fulfilling the success criteria of the arts college development plan. Specialist school status has enabled the art department to employ many more artists in residence and fund art projects which are currently providing a rich new experience for our pupils whilst also extending the expertise and pedagogical approach of the art staff. We have been able to fund cross curricular and cross phase projects and to form strong links with local art groups and galleries. All of this work has been undertaken with the express intention of developing new approaches to the teaching of art at St Paul's Way Community School.

The erased drawing project, undertaken with Camerawork by a group of year 10 pupils was our first step towards introducing a issues based work into the department's repertoire. The project, although not entirely successful, did serve to highlight for us the need for considerable reflection upon how a conceptual element could be introduced into our teaching. The biggest issue raised during the project was how to undertake work which whilst strong on ideas, still motivated pupils through enabling a quality outcome to the final product. The project as delivered by Camerawork probably did not conform to our accepted view of what a GCSE project might be. I was happy to let the artists take control of the delivery of the project, if concerned about the pupils attitudes to the outcomes of their work and their perception of what they were experiencing. Pupils' lack of confidence in their work was highlighted in their questioning of the worth of the work produced. Time and again I was asked: What grade will it get at GCSE? There was clearly a lack of understanding regarding the aims of the project. From the teachers' point of view, there was a degree of skepticism. We observed pupils who would, given past performance, undoubtedly achieve highly at GCSE, producing work which they, (and we), felt was poor technically and on which the children appeared to have few points of reference upon which to base a judgment of personal satisfaction.

As the school sessions progressed my colleagues and I began to detect that pupils felt the artists were imposing the work upon them rather than allowing them to embark upon an individual investigation of the project. Explanations by Camerawork of the underpinning concepts of the project were not always immediately accessible to young people who for many English is spoken as an additional language. The pupils told us that making a drawing and then in their terms destroying it seemed a strange thing to do, particularly when they were asked to redraw over the erasing. Previous experience of making art had obviously pre-programmed them to see erasure as a device for correction. Now, being encouraged to use erasers to actively 'destroy' a piece of work threw some pupils into a flat spin.

At the conclusion of the erased drawing, pupils visited Camerawork gallery participating in a range of activities connected to the work completed in school. Here several more adults were available to work with the pupils in small groups on specific tasks. This day long session was much more successful than the school-based projects. Pupils interacted with the Camerawork staff and gradually through explanation and practical activities became more aware of the central issues of the project.

With hindsight, as most of our pupils come from families with cultural backgrounds other than European we now feel it doubly important with this type of work to explain extremely carefully the background references and issues to the project set within an intellectual construct which accounted for and made reference to their own experience of art making. In short, to use the best practice which we employ as a matter of course for our 'normal' art activities. This approach, regularly reinforced orally and utilising carefully structured practical activities and homework research would serve to counter any lack of understanding of the theoretical base of the project. We will incorporate an issues-based element into our schemes of work in the near future but we will temper this with the best of our current practice to create a balanced curriculum which enables our pupils to achieve highly producing work with intellectual rigour and practical excellence.

Erased Drawings, and documentation by Honufa Bibi, 1997.

Putting up/taking down "School Is a Factory", from Allan Sekula's exhibition, Dismal Science, Camerawork, London, Oct. - Nov. 1997.

from School Is a Factory, Allan Sekula

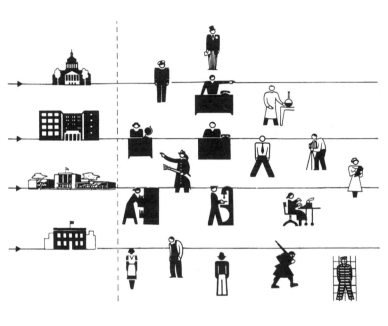

"Our schools are, in a sense, factories in which the raw materials are to be shaped and fashioned into products to meet the various demands of life. The specifications for manufacturing come from the demands of the twentieth-century civilization, and it is the business of the school to build its pupils to the specifications laid down."
Ellwood Cubberly, *Public School Administration,* 1916.

[...] This essay is a deliberate provocation, less an intervention from some fictitious 'outside' world than an argument from within.

In the 'developed' world, school and media bring a formidable play of forces to bear upon the self, transforming and supplanting the more traditional patriarchal authority that emanated from religion and family in the epochs of feudalism and entrepreneurial capitalism. Both mass schooling and mass media are developments intrinsic and necessary to the corporate capitalist world order that emerged in the very late nineteenth and early twentieth centuries. In the United States, the decade after the First World War saw the triumph of a new national culture, a 'business' culture, reproduced through compulsory education and promulgated by mass circulation periodicals, radio and the movies. These forces sought to organise people as atomised 'private individuals,' motivated en masse by the prospect of consumption, thus liquidating other dangerously oppositional forms of social bonding based on class, sex, race and ethnicity.

We have been led by the champions of corporate liberalism to believe that schooling and the media are instruments of freedom.

1. The complete version of this text was first published in Allan Sekula, *Photography against the Grain: Essays and Photo Works 1973-1983*, Halifax, Nova Scotia: Press of the Nova Scotia College of Art and Design, 1984, now out of print, and has been republished in Allan Sekula, *Dismal Science: Photo Works 1972-1996*, Normal, Illinois: Illinois State University, 1999.

Accordingly, these institutions are seen to fulfil the democratic promise of the Enlightenment by bringing knowledge and upward social mobility within reach of everyone, by allowing each individual to reach his or her limits. This ideology hides the relentless sorting function performed by school and media. Both institutions serve to legitimate and reproduce a strict hierarchy of power relations, tracking individuals into places in a complex social division of labour while suggesting that we have only ourselves to blame for our failures. School and the media effectively situate most people in a culture and economy over which they have no control, and thus are mechanisms by which an 'enlightened' few promote the subtle silencing of the many.[2]

School and the media are inherently discursive institutions, sites within which discourse becomes a locus of symbolic force, of symbolic violence. A communicative relation is established between teacher and student, performer and audience, in which the first part, as the purveyor of official 'truths,' exerts an institutional authority over the second. Students and audience are reduced to the status of passive listeners, rather than active subjects of knowledge. Resistance is almost always limited only to the possibility of tuning out. Domination depends on a monologue of sorts, a 'conversation' in which one party names and directs the other, while the other listens deferentially, docilely, resentfully, perhaps full of suppressed rage. When the wholly dominated listener turns to speak, it is with the internalised voice of the master. This is the dynamic of all oppressions of race, gender, and class. All dominating power functions semiotically through the naming of the other as subordinate, dependent, incomplete as a human being without the master's discipline and support. Clearly, such relationships can be overthrown; the discourse of domination finds its dialectical antagonist in a discourse and practice of liberation. Like home, factory, prison and city streets, school and the media are sites of an intense, if often covert, daily struggle in which language and power are inextricably connected.[3]

2. Clearly, an adequate account of the developments alluded to in the last two paragraphs would require volumes.[...]
3. See Paulo Freire's *Pedagogy of the Oppressed*, New York, 1970, for a very important dialectical understanding of the educational process in its dominating and liberating modes. Ira Schor's *Critical Teaching and Everyday Life*, Boston 1980, does an admirable job of translating Freire's insights concerning peasant

Most of us who have managed to develop a professional relation to the traffic in words and images (as artists, writers, or teachers) share, often unequally and competitively, in a *symbolic privilege* which situates us above whole populations of the silenced and voiceless. This role, the role of cultural mouthpiece, normally partakes in the privileging and accreditation of its own status, and that of its patrons and employers, while suggesting that culture exists for everyone, or for its own sake. A contradiction has developed between the bureaucratic and professional organisation of all cultural work and the Janus-faced mythology of culture, which suggests, on the one hand, that mass culture is popular and democratic, while arguing, on the other, that high culture is an elite activity, and Olympian conversation between genius and connoisseur. High culture is increasingly no more than a specialised and pretentious variant of mass culture, speaking to an audience composed of the upper class and the intermediary strata of professionals and managers (and especially those professionals and managers whose business is culture). The star system prevails in both SoHo and Hollywood: all culture becomes publicity, a matter of exposure.[4]

But artists and intellectuals do not control the interlocking apparatuses of culture and education. Increasingly they are the functionaries and employees of corporate and state institutions: primarily as teachers and grant recipients. The ideology of autonomous professionalism serves to legitimate and defend career interests while, particularly in the case of artist-teachers, building on a hollow legacy of romantic individualism. Although the myth of the lonely oppositional path retains its redemptive ideological force, artists are forced into a dreary upwardly-mobile competition for visibility, with reputation translating into career-capital. Those who refuse or fail are officially invisible, without voice. (I once heard a well-known artist characterise less well-known artists, generally, as lazy.)

societies into terms compatible with the experience of North American working-class students. Pierre Bourdieu's and Jean-Claude Passeron's *Reproduction*, London, 1977, is theoretically dense but valuable in its attempt at a "theory of symbolic violence" in the pedagogical sphere. Adrienne Rich's essays on education in *On Lies, Secrets, and Silence*, New York, 1979, especially the one entitled "Toward a Woman-Centred University," are among the most lucid statements I have read on the radical remaking of educational possibilities,....
4. [...]

[...] Very few teachers acknowledge the constraints placed on their would-be *auteurs* by a system of educational tracking based on class, race, and sex.

Thus, most of us who teach, or make art, or go to school with a desire to do these things, are forced to accept that a winner's game requires losers. One can either embrace this proposition with a social-Darwinist steeling of the nerves, or pretend that it is not true while trying to survive anyway. Otherwise we might begin to work for a method of education and a culture based on a struggle for social equality. [...]

AN OPEN CONCLUSION

The celebration, by ruling class commissions, of universal art education, of art education as the 'Fourth R' in a revamped, redecorated system of schooling, must be questioned when the same ruling class is promoting educational cutbacks at the same time.[5] When functional literacy rates are declining, what does it mean to promote a massive shift of educational attention to the development of the aesthetic faculties? This plan reads like a technocratic perversion of the liberating pedagogy envisioned by the German Romantic poet Schiller in his 1793 letters *On the Aesthetic Education of Man*.[6] The aestheticism encouraged by the cultural bureaucrats of the 1980s stops short of a necessary integration with critical consciousness. Rather, what seems to have taken shape in these plans is a technocratic vision of a society of expressionist *units*, playing happily as consumers (of less and less) in a world in which political life is increasingly limited to a spectacle of representation. The task of progressive teachers, artists, and students is to critique this vision and combat its further realisation, while preserving the awareness that utopian aesthetic possibilities must be struggled for as intrinsic to a genuinely democratic future, but cannot be achieved in a society governed by a mechanical and world-threatening lust for profit and control.

---

5. [...]
6. Friedrich Schiller, *On the Aesthetic Education of Man*, New York, 1977. See also Herbert Marcuse, "The Aesthetic Dimension", in *Eros and Civilisation*, Boston, 1955.

unpicking texts from Allan Sekula's exhibition Dismal Science, Camerawork, Dec. 1997.

85

NOTES ON CONTRIBUTORS:

Nicholas Addison is Lecturer in Art Education, Institute of Education, University of London.

Rajia Begum is a school-student at St. Paul's Way Community School, London.

Honufa Bibi is a school-student at St. Paul's Way Community School, London.

Tim Brennan is an artist and Assistant Programme Director for the MA Fine Art Administration and Curatorship at Goldsmiths College, University of London.

Geoff Cox is an artist and formerly Education Programmer at Camerawork gallery and currently Senior Lecturer in Media Arts, University of Plymouth.

David Davies is Head of Visual Arts, St. Paul's Way Community School, London.

Howard Hollands is Principal Lecturer in Art & Design Education, Middlesex University.

Sydul Islam is a school-student at St. Paul's Way Community School, London.

Shubead Miah is a school-student at St. Paul's Way Community School, London.

Victoria de Rijke is Senior Lecturer in Education, Literature and Performing Arts, Middlesex University.

Allan Sekula is an artist and writer based in Los Angeles.